Od mamičky 1989.

MEDIEVAL ART

Medieval Art

Decorative fowl. Book of Kells. Irish, late 8th cent.

Text and Notes by
SHARON GALLAGHER

TUDOR PUBLISHING COMPANY
New York

TUDOR PUBLISHING COMPANY
New York, 1969
Library of Congress Catalog Card Number: 68–30735
Printed in Japan

MEDIEVAL ART

PAINTING, MOSAICS, MANUSCRIPTS, ENAMELS, STAINED GLASS

What we call Medieval Art is largely that of Europe during the Middle Ages, a loosely applied term which encompasses many territories and periods. But it is united, as its art shows, by an ordered spiritual realm of common belief, the Christian faith. Medieval art is predominantly the art of this faith, and its chief patron, for over a thousand years, is the church. After the collapse of the military order of the Roman Empire, it was the spiritual order centered in the church that was to organize and build a rich, flourishing civilization that reached its peak in Europe in the twelfth and thirteenth centuries.

In all this, Byzantium plays a special and mighty role. In many ways a separate, static and local culture, the Eastern Roman Empire is also the mother and transmitter of much that we call Medieval. It directly influenced not only the art of Greece, Russia and Armenia, but of Italy as well, as Venice and Ravenna bear witness. Less directly, through trade, and the reverse cultural impact of the crusades, it planted the seeds of the styles which, transformed by local influences, became Romanesque and Gothic.

EARLY CHRISTIAN ART

The European political unity known as Medieval Europe did not replace the disintegrating Roman Empire until the eighth century, when Charlemagne laid claim to the old territory under a new name, the Holy Roman Empire. But well before that, even during the peak of Roman power, a Christian spiritual realm existed side by side with the pagan culture. The earliest surviving Christian art dates from the third and fourth centuries, the paintings and mosaics of the

5

catacombs (1–3), secret images of a persecuted sect. Later, after 334 A.D., when Constantine made Christianity the official state religion, hundreds of churches were built and filled with a splendid array of mosaics, paintings and sacred objects. This first phase of the Medieval tradition is known as Early Christian.

Early Christian art developed directly from pagan prototypes. In the illusionistic manner of Roman painting, the aim was to make a convincing recreation of visual reality. Proportions were naturalistic, figures and draperies´ were modelled in light and shade, and represented with softly blended, muted colors (3, 6, 7, 11). Nevertheless, the Roman Christian tended to withdraw from the external, materialistic world toward a new inner meaning—the eternal life of the soul through Christ. At first, Christian art carried this deeper meaning only through symbolism. Grape vines stood for the wine of the Eucharist (2); the peacock (13) was a symbol of Paradise or the immortality of the soul. Other scenes used traditional realism to portray instructional episodes from the Bible.

The fusion of pagan and Christian concepts can also be seen in Coptic art, the art of Christian Egypt (4, 5). Here, the Greco-Roman influence is so strong that a pagan deity such as Dionysos is shown with a Christian halo (4).

BYZANTIUM

In 323 A.D. Constantine the Great moved the capital of the Roman Empire to the Greek town of Byzantium, renaming it Constantinople (present day Istanbul). This fateful move, which set up for the first time since Carthage a political rival to Rome, was to divide the Empire, a division soon solidified by a theological dispute for primacy culminating in the Great Schism and resulting in the Eastern or Orthodox church.

Furthermore, while the Roman Catholic Church claimed the authority of St. Peter and independence of the state, the Eastern church was dominated by the Emperor himself, who claimed authority directly as the "Vicar of God." Thus Byzantium was a theocracy, uniting the spiritual and the secular, and throughout its long history was free of the quarrels between Emperor and

Pope that characterize Medieval history in the West. This stability was both its glory and its downfall. It produced great art, but also static and repetitive art which long outlasted its vitality.

Once considered a minor and relatively insignificant culture, Byzantium has been increasingly recognized as a great civilization. It created many of the basic elements of Christian art, its color, directness and freedom from naturalistic bonds. Moreover, because it was able to resist the Germanic migratory invasions that disrupted civilization in the West, it retained a secure hold on its Greco-Hellenistic heritage. Byzantine culture was the last legacy of the Greeks and Romans to the Western world, a stabilizing force and reservoir of literary and artistic sources which were eventually to inspire the beginnings of the Renaissance in fourteenth-century Italy (87, 88).

THE ART OF BYZANTIUM

Byzantine art can be divided into three periods. Under the reign of the emperor Justinian (527–565), a tremendous artistic and architectural campaign was launched, which began the Golden Age of Byzantine art. This was to last until the end of the ninth century, when a century-long series of theological clashes (the Iconoclast Crises) resulted in the temporary banning of religious images. A second period of greatness flourished under the Macedonian and Comnene emperors (9th–12 centuries). The third and last period, called the Palaeologue Renaissance (13th–15th centuries), ended with the capture and destruction of Constantinople by the Turks in 1453.

During the first Golden Age of Byzantium, the Justinian Age, the rich, resplendent court style was created. Centered in Constantinople, it radiated to other provinces, particularly Italy and the city of Ravenna, then under Byzantine dominance. Thus, though Constantinople was later destroyed and largely stripped, Ravenna still preserves rich and important examples of Byzantine splendor (10, 13, 14, 15, 16, 17). Possibly the style in the capital was more purely classical, as a rare fifth- or sixth-century pavement mosaic (11) from the Palace of the Emperors suggests. By comparing this mosaic to those in Ravenna, particularly to a detail from San Vitale representing Moses (14), we can clearly

7

see a continuation of the classical heritage. Naturalistic proportions with contours of figure and drapery are emphasized by dark and light contrasts. However, the Ravenna figure is flattened, with greater emphasis on its outline. The predominant difference is color; a dazzling, rich display of gold and bright luminous stones characterizes the new Byzantine style, a reminder of the Near Eastern love of decoration and precious materials.

The mosaics of S. Maria Maggiore in Rome (12), done about 430 A.D., are similar to those in Ravenna. As yet there is no clear distinction between early Christian and Byzantine art. Both show similarities of style and iconography; they make frequent use of symbols and favor narrative illustrations from the Old Testament (3, 12, 14).

Byzantine painting also derives from the classical. A Madonna and Christ Child from Mt. Sinai (8), done on wood, is executed in an ancient technique which builds up layers of paint to suggest the visual world of light and shadow. Yet the image assumes a sanctity and other-worldliness which is to begin a long tradition of holy images called *icons*. This sixth- or seventh-century work may be compared with icons from the tenth and eleventh centuries (40, 41). The flattened pose, fixed outline and large staring eyes create an image far removed from the changing world of external events (8, 9, 10). Art has begun to suggest the inner, eternal realm of the spirit.

After the reign of Justinian, and throughout the seventh century, Byzantine art declined, and was finally interrupted by the Iconoclast controversy. Because the image had taken on a sacredness hardly distinguished from that of the holy or divine person represented, the exaggerated importance of artistic representation produced a reaction. An imperial edict of 726 prohibited all religious images. Statues disappeared and numerous images were destroyed.

During the second great period of Byzantine art (9th–12th centuries), scholars and artists turned directly to works of Greek and Roman antiquity. In the Paris Psalter (Constantinople, 10th century, Plate 34), we see an architectural background with cast shadows, and the figure is given a voluminous, three-dimensional quality—all of which is closer to Roman illusionism than to the flat, abstract art of the early Byzantine period.

But the majority of artistic products of this period come from outlying areas of Byzantium, where the older Byzantine tradition still prevails, under a more strictly theological, rather than courtly, cast. During these centuries

Byzantine art spread not only into such Western centers as Venice (21, 22, 32, 33), but also into Greece (19), Bulgaria (28), Armenia (35), Cappadocia (23, 24), Serbia (25, 26) and Russia (40, 41). That is, everywhere that the Orthodox religion has been adopted. Monasticism is a major influence in this dissemination. Even in Constantinople itself monastic artists tended toward a more severe and theological approach, with subject matter and even manner of execution under strict, dogmatic control. Figures lose their corporeality, space becomes abstract and a linear style replaces the pictorial (23, 24, 25). A greater moral earnestness and spirituality become apparent, as Byzantine masters convey the holiness of saints through a sense of their inner being. Although possibly of a later period, the mosaic of Christ in Hagia Sophia, Constantinople, which radiates an awesome grandeur, is a masterpiece of this tendency (20).

Mosaics continued to be one of the major forms of Byzantine art (19–22). But far from being merely decorative, they were intimately bound up with the fundamental concept of the church as a divine building, which mystically embodied the impalpable realities of the Christian faith. Often images were connected with the liturgy. But even when they were not, they participated merely by their presence, deriving importance and sanctity from their location in the grand scheme of divine symbolism.

In the twelfth century, under the Comnene emperors, a new spirit of expression may be seen. Influenced by the personal, emotional hymns of Symeon Metaphrastes, artists created images of Christ and the saints full of compassion and tenderness. In the wall paintings of Nerez (25) powerfully expressive faces and gestures convey the most intimate grief and poignancy.

THE LAST BYZANTINE PHASE

The conquest of Constantinople by the crusaders in 1204 destroyed the main cultural center of Byzantium, though it also spread Eastern influences to the West. In 1261 the city was reconquered by the Greek emperor Michael Palaeologus, who revived the Empire for the last time. The last phase of Byzantine art (13th–15th centuries) is known as the Palaeologue Renaissance.

9

Works from earlier periods were frequently imitated or copied. But the rigorous ordering and monumentality of the Middle Byzantine gave way to a more narrative, graceful and touchingly human quality (28, 42, 43). On the whole, frescos replaced mosaics, and icons became the predominant art form. An icon of the Annunciation from Yugoslavia is one of the finest examples (43 and cover). The revival of classical antiquity can be seen in the attempt to create pictorial space. The slender forms, fine details, active poses and fluttering drapery all give a refined, lively delicacy.

During this period the Orthodox religion and Byzantine art spread to new territories in Turkey, Greece and Russia. Also, Rumanian art is born (28, 29). It is in these outlying areas that Byzantine art is to survive the final destruction of the Eastern Empire in 1453.

ART IN THE WEST—THE DARK AGES

While the history of Byzantine art displays a consistency and an unbroken link with antiquity, culture in the West after the fall of Rome is disrupted for several centuries, the so-called "Dark Ages." The waves of barbarian migrations that had helped to weaken the empire are followed in the fifth and sixth centuries by still other wanderings. Pagan Germanic peoples drifted from central Asia and northwest Europe toward new homes in the south and west, where they gradually adopted Christianity and formed the cultural and linguistic nuclei of modern Europe.

The art of these folk consisted mainly of goldsmith's work and carved stone monuments (46, 47). Decoration shows a tendency for complex, abstract, linear designs. Unlike the Byzantines, for whom the human figure was the most important element, the barbarians preferred fanciful linear ornament with some anthropomorphic and animal forms.

The Celts, who occupied the British Isles before the Anglo-Saxon invasions, may have been influenced by the Scythians, Near Eastern experts in metalwork. Celtic art is known for its fantastic vocabulary of curves, countercurves, spirals and interlaces. After the Saxon conquest, Germanic elements combined with Celtic ones in a style called Hiberno-Saxon, which flourished in monasteries founded by Irishmen in Saxon England from the seventh to tenth centuries (48–51). The whole grammar of abstract art was employed to embellish sacred texts. A page from the Book of Kells (50) resembles jewelry in its rich profusion of colorful linear designs. Even after the Norman invasion, Hiberno-Saxon influences continued in English manuscript initials (53, 54). The style was widely diffused by Irish monks who established monasteries throughout Europe, where it became an important element in many local styles.

THE CAROLINGIAN RENAISSANCE

By the end of the eighth century, Western Europe was poised on the edge of a new cultural synthesis. The classical and Early Christian worlds had been largely destroyed and swept away by the barbarian invasions. The Byzantine tradition in the East, while strong, failed to exercise effective political control west of the Adriatic. Yet all these traditions were to play significant roles in the development of the new cultural heritage that begins with Charlemagne and culminates in the Romanesque and Gothic periods.

In the year 800, Charlemagne, an obscure chief who had inherited the kingdom of the Franks in 768, was crowned Holy Roman Emperor by Pope Leo III. By the force of his extraordinary personality, he created in a brief fourteen years the foundation of a new civilization. The Carolingian Renaissance, which flourished in the major political and religious centers of the empire, was directly inspired by the imperial court—a conscious attempt to force culture and learning upon an illiterate amalgamation of barbarian peoples. Art and architecture were important to Charlemagne for conveying to the Frankish people, who lacked a wide cultural background, an idea of the empire he was trying to revive. But the renascence surpassed its political inspiration. Scholars and artists were recruited from as far away as Ireland, and a great period of building, artistic productivity and learning was initiated. Nor was the "renaissance" only a looking back to Roman and Byzantine cultures. Many local traditions contributed as well. While there was a conscious revival of the antique in manuscripts, for example, Carolingian artists were inspired by many other sources, especially the Hiberno-Saxon or Insular school (57, 59).

11

The Saxon rulers of the succeeding Ottonian dynasty furthered the political aims and artistic ideas of the Carolingians. The period, which takes its name from the three emperors called Otto, began with the imperial coronation of Otto I in 962 and lasted until the death of Henry III in 1056. Because of its close connection with the Eastern court, Byzantine influence was strong. However, the major source was Carolingian (60, 61). The Gospel book of Otto III shows Otto as the Holy Roman Emperor in the tradition of Charlemagne, but portrays him as ruler of both the political and ecclesiastical realms, a Byzantine tradition. Yet, Ottonian art developed new creative expressions and a more monumental style which was to lay the foundations for the next phase of Western Medieval art.

THE RISE OF ROMANESQUE

At the end of the tenth century Magyar and Viking raids ceased to be a threat. Trade routes reopened and a general era of peace was accompanied by an architectural renaissance which spread throughout Europe. As these buildings were based on Roman methods of construction—the round arch and massive stone vaults—the style was called Romanesque. Arts and letters were revived in the great abbeys, pilgrimage centers and canonical churches. As Romanesque art flourished throughout the Christian world during the eleventh century and much of the twelfth, a great variety of types and styles proliferated. Romanesque art derives largely from Carolingian and Ottonian prototypes, but many other traditions were absorbed. There was the everpresent background of Roman, Early Christian and Byzantine (71), and in some areas influences came from barbarian, Oriental and Moslem art (66).

In manuscript illumination (66, 67, 68, 69, 70) and wall paintings (71, 72, 73, 75), which replaced mosaics as wall decoration inside churches, there tended to be a more schematic style with greater exaggerations of the figure than in the preceding Carolingian and Ottonian periods. This was all far removed from classic naturalism. Compare, for instance, a Spanish fresco of the twelfth century (75) with an Early Christian catacomb painting (1) or an Ottonian manuscript (61). The Romanesque example is broken into brightly colored and boldly outlined shapes which hold together more decoratively than naturalistically.

Art flourished in many media and reflected cultural events as well as Biblical themes. The Bayeux tapestry, which illustrates the Norman invasion of England, is a rare example of history woven into a splendid pictorial narrative. Another example, a tapestry from Baldishol portraying a knight, reminds us that the twelfth century was an era of crusades and chivalry.

Mosan art used a technique of creating pictorial images in enamel fused with metal (62, 63, 64, 65). It flourished in the Walloon provinces and developed in Lorraine, penetrating into Austria, Poland, Switzerland and Scandinavia. It was influenced by Ottonian goldsmith work as well as by an older barbarian tradition of small jewel-like work in metal. Mosan work remained imperial in its patronage. Perhaps it is through imperial models as well as ancient remains that Mosan artists were able to study classical forms. The fluid, naturalistic style had considerable influence on Gothic sculpture. The twelfth-century enamel shoulder pads depicting the Resurrection of Christ, with its graceful relaxed style of drawing, anticipates the elegance of Gothic naturalism.

GOTHIC

The last period of Medieval art, called Gothic, was an uninterrupted continuation of civilization in the 12th century. The term Gothic refers i ʾainly to an architectural style. The innovations of the pointed, ribbed vault permitted a lighter, taller building with a different spatial arrangement. The new style radiated from the Île-de-France to the large cities of northern France and from there to all of Europe. The development of cathedral cities accompanied the flowering of civilization on all levels. The heavy, secluded monastic style of the twelfth century gave way to an urbane flowering of elegance and sophistication. While the Romanesque style varied greatly according to region, the Gothic was a more homogeneous and international style.

The Gothic style of building began with the church of St. Denis, erected between 1137 and 1144. The abbot of the church, Suger, brought artisans from many different regions. Architects, sculptors, and stained-glass and metal workers were to combine their arts in a way that had never been done before. Suger wanted great areas of window space for stained glass. Inspired by writings of the pseudo-Dionysius, a Platonist, Suger saw the brilliantly colored light of the cathedral as symbolic of the divine light of God. Number too was symbolic, thus part related to part in a theory of proportions to create the perfect harmony. Many other buildings were then built in a similar style. After the pointed arch, the flying buttress was developed to permit higher structures in which greater areas could be devoted to stained glass (80, 81, 82, 83, 84).

The relaxed, naturalistic sculpture and paintings of the Gothic period were executed with fluid lines, flowing drapery, and figures modelled with a greater sense of volume (82, 83). The powerful monarchies closely allied with the church further encouraged the chivalric spirit, as did the religious crusades of the thirteenth century. The importance of the Virgin Mary and courtly love influenced tastes for delicacy and fashionable elegance in the late thirteenth century and especially during the fourteenth (89, 91).

In Italy during the thirteenth and fourteenth centuries a new influx of late Byzantine art inspired artists to create a monumental figural style in painting that is closer to the classical Roman period than anything done since then in the West (87, 88). While this movement led to the Renaissance in Italy in the fifteenth century, the Gothic style continued elsewhere in Europe until as late as the sixteenth century.

THE MEDIEVAL SYNTHESIS

The variety and inventiveness of Medieval art owes much to the interchange and confrontation of two legacies: the classical tradition of figurative art and the Near Eastern love of color and abstract design. Greco-Roman art, although often submerged, never died out. Classical prototypes were admired, repeatedly imitated and incorporated into existing local styles, especially in those areas which maintained an uninterrupted link with the past, such as the old Roman capital of Constantinople.

The art of the Near East, with its strong love for the decorative, flowed into Europe through Constantinople or was brought by the migratory peoples from Central Asia. Egypt, with its hieroglyphic writing, made familiar an art which fused picture with symbol. In some instances the influence can be traced directly. A Coptic textile depicts water with decorative symbols of fish and plants in an Egyptian fashion that goes back to the Old Kingdom (5). A Byzantine silk uses motifs from the Sassanian Persians (45). More often, the Oriental influence is indirect and transformed, as in the rich decoration of the Archangel Michael from the Homilies of St. John Chrysostom (37).

Catalyzed by the Christian faith, with its otherworldly bent, its new iconography and need to glorify God, these two traditions blended to produce the changing variety of Medieval art. Because classical standards of beauty have predominated since the Renaissance, it is only in the last few decades that this art has come to be widely appreciated. Motivated primarily by faith, Medieval art has often reached the heights of forceful expressiveness and inspired fantasy of spirit. Its rich decoration, brilliant coloring and directness of form, its charming disregard of the limits of classical naturalism, give it a freshness, sincerity and beauty that we are only now beginning to discover.

IMPORTANT DATES

306	After the abdication of Diocletian, Constantine I, "The Great," (288–337) lays claim to the Roman throne.
313	Constantine converts to Christianity after a cross in the sky (according to Eusebius) guides him to victory. Becomes the first Christian Roman Emperor.
4th–5th cents.	The Huns invade Europe, and under Attila control most of what is now Germany, Poland and European Russia. Forays of Goths and Vandals into Italy, Spain and Southern France weaken the heart of the Roman Empire.
323	The capital of the Empire is transferred by Constantine to Byzantium, which is renamed Constantinople. The division of the Empire begins.
325	The Nicene Council—first of a long series of general Church councils to define doctrine, continuing to the present day.
334	Constantine proclaims Christianity the official state religion.
380	Emperor Theodosius I confirms Christianity as the official religion of the Eastern Empire.
381	The Council of Constantinople elaborates the Nicene Creed and condemns Apollinarism, a heresy directed against the divinity of Christ.
Ca. 385	Birth of St. Patrick.
410	Visigoths invade Italy and sack Rome.
413–26	St. Augustine writes *De civitate Dei*.
Ca. 430	Mosaics of S. Maria Maggiore in Rome.
Ca. 450	Anglo-Saxons begin migrations from the Continent to Britain.
451	Rome is sacked by the Vandal Genseric.
476	Romulus Augustulus, the last Western Roman emperor, resigns his throne to Odoacer, a Danubian German.

481	Clovis founds the Frankish Kingdom.

481 Clovis founds the Frankish Kingdom.

488 Ostrogoths invade Italy under Theodoric and establish a kingdom (destroyed in 552–5 by Justinian I).

526–47 Church of San Vitale, Ravenna.

527–47 Reign of Justinian I, inaugurating the First Golden Age of Byzantine civilization.

532–37 Cathedral of Hagia Sophia, Constantinople.

534–39 Sant'Apollinare, Ravenna.

568 Lombards conquer northern Italy, and found the kingdom of Lombardy (overthrown by Charlemagne in 774).

570 Birth of Mohammed in Mecca.

711 Saracens invade Spain and establish the Moorish Kingdom, which lasts until 1492.

726, 730 The first two Iconoclast decrees ban religious images in Byzantium. Icons are not officially restored until 843.

Ca. 731 The Venerable Bede writes the *Ecclesiastical History of the English People*.

732 Charles Martel, ruler of the Franks, defeats the Saracens near Poitiers, France, checking the Moorish thrust in the West.

800 Charlemagne crowned Emperor of the West on Christmas day. Establishes the Holy Roman Empire in an attempt to revive the Roman imperial tradition. Beginning of the Carolingian Renaissance.

Ca. 800 *Book of Kells.*

867–1057 The Macedonian dynasty inaugurated by Basil I, under whose reign Byzantine culture begins its Second Golden Age.

871 Alfred the Great of England contains the threat of Danish occupation, establishes a center of learning and inspires the compilation of the *Anglo-Saxon Chronicle*.

955 Otto I, "The Great," repels the invasion of the Magyars and Slavs; becomes Holy Roman Emperor (962–73) and unites the crowns of Germany and Italy.

Ca. 998	*Gospel book of Otto III.*
Ca. 1000	Leif Ericson's Vikings reach Vinland.
1046	Emperor Henry III deposes contending popes for the see of Peter and appoints his own. Beginning of long struggle for supremacy between Empire and Papacy.
1054	The Great Schism results in the final split between the Eastern and Western Churches.
1063	Construction begun on Cathedral of St. Mark, Venice.
1066	Norman Conquest of England. William the Conquerer defeats the English at Hastings.
Ca. 1080	The Bayeux Tapestry.
1096–99	First Crusade. Jerusalem captured, 1099.
Ca. 1100	*Chanson de Roland.*
12th–16th cents.	Mont-Saint-Michel.
Ca. 1136	*Historia calamitatum* of Peter Abelard.
1137–44	Construction of Abbey of St. Denis, prototype of the Gothic style.
1147–9	Second Crusade, preached by St. Bernard of Clairvaux. Fails in attempt to capture Damascus.
1152	Frederick Barbarossa elected Holy Roman Emperor. Establishes a powerful monarchy in Central Europe.
1162–76	Frederick captures Milan (1162) and Rome (1166), but is defeated by the Lombard League and driven from Italy in 1176.
1163	Construction begun on Cathedral of Notre Dame, Paris.
1170	St. Thomas Becket murdered in Canterbury Cathedral.
1187	Saladin, Sultan of Egypt and Syria, captures Jerusalem, precipitating the Third Crusade.
Ca. 1193	Birth of Albertus Magnus, who worked to bring about the union of Aristotelianism and Christian theology, the basis of Scholasticism.

1194	Construction begun on main part of Chartres Cathedral. (The Old Spire, façade and West Portal date from 1145–65.)
1202–4	Fourth Crusade. The Crusaders conquer Constantinople, which becomes the capital of a Latin Empire. (Recaptured by the Greek Emperor Michael Palaeologue in 1261.)
1209	The Albigensian Crusade—slaughter of an heretical sect in southern France. In Italy, St. Francis of Assisi founds the Franciscan Order, which produces many of the leading Medieval scholars.
Ca. 1212	St. Dominic founds the Dominican Order to convert the Albigenses. Children's Crusade, 1212.
1215	The "Papacy Triumphant." Fourth Latern Council, convened by Innocent III, unifies Western Christendom. Commencement of age of papal glory and power. Magna Carta signed by King John at Runnymede.
1218–21	Fifth Crusade, against the Saracens in Egypt, fails. Sixth Crusade (1228–9), led by Emperor Frederick II, secures Jerusalem, Bethlehem and Nazareth by treaty. Seventh Crusade (1248–54) is proclaimed by Pope Innocent IV after the capture of Jerusalem by the Saracens.
1240	Birth of Cimabue.
1250–1350	The Alhambra, palace of the Moorish kings at Granada.
1261–1453	Palaeologue Renaissance, the final flowering of Byzantine culture.
1267	Birth of Giotto.
1267–73	St. Thomas Aquinas writes *Summa Theologica*.
1270	Eighth Crusade, led by Louis IX of France and resulting in his death, ends in failure.
Ca. 1300	Birth of Guillaume de Machault, composer of the "Notre Dame Mass," a monument of Medieval music.
1308–20	Dante's *Divine Comedy*.
1309–76	"Babylonian Captivity." Papacy is removed to Avignon, where it is dominated by the French kings.
1337–1453	Hundred Years' War—intermittent hostilities between France and England weaken feudalism.
Ca. 1340	Birth of Chaucer.

1347–50	The "Black Death" (bubonic plague). Millions dead.
1378–1417	The Great Schism of the later Middle Ages. Rival Popes in Rome and Avignon.
Ca. 1381	Tapestry of Angers.
1382	John Wycliffe directs first translation of the Vulgate Bible into English vernacular.
1414–18	Council of Constance resolves the Great Schism. The Church is reformed and the Papacy reestablished in Rome.
1415	English victorious under Henry V at the Battle of Agincourt. Nation states of France and England begin to emerge.
1429	Joan of Arc leads the French to victory at Orleans and has Charles VII crowned King of France. She is burned at Rouen for heresy in 1431.
1453	Capture and destruction of Constantinople by the Turks, and collapse of the Byzantine Empire.

NOTES ON THE COLOR PLATES

1. *Veiled Orant.* Wall painting. *Ca.* 220–40 A.D. Catacomb of St. Priscilla, Rome. The orant, or praying figure, is done in a style close to that of contemporary secular paintings in Rome, except that, as in most catacomb painting, the brushwork is lighter and sketchier. The ancient Greeks and Romans prayed to their gods with arms raised and outstretched, a custom which was followed by the early Christians.

2. *Christ as Apollo the Sun God (Christos Helios).* Mosaic. 3rd cent. A.D. Necropolis under St. Peter's, Rome. Remnants of ancient non-Hellenic sun worship had already been associated with the Greek deity Apollo, who raced across the sky in his golden chariot. After the advent of Christianity, pagan and Christian images were fused and Christ became the new symbol of divine radiance. The decorative grape vines symbolize the wine of the Eucharist. Mosaics had long been in use in the Roman world.

3. *Three Youths in the Furnace.* Wall painting. 3rd–4th cents. A.D. Catacomb of St. Priscilla, Rome. Roman illusionism often used a quick, painterly, spontaneous technique, which has been adopted in this catacomb painting. The brief, impressionistic strokes seem especially suited to the dramatic action of the story. Like the orant in (1), the figures are shown in an attitude of prayer.

4. *Coptic textile with Dionysos.* 4th–6th cents. A.D. (Kunsthistorisches Museum, Vienna.) From the first dynasties, Egyptian art had fused picture with symbol in a severe stylization which was often beautifully ornamental. The tendency was in marked contrast with the naturalism of Hellenistic art. Christianity in Egypt, as elsewhere, was readily adopted by the lower classes, who rejected the Hellenistic culture of the refined upper classes in favor of the traditional style. Yet the two were frequently combined. Thus, the pagan god with a "Christian" halo is set in a decorative border.

5. *Coptic textile with Figures and Fish.* 4th–6th cents. (Louvre, Paris.) The hot, dry sands of Egypt have miraculously preserved a number of examples of these highly ornamented fabrics. Here, the traditional symbols for the Nile or water may have taken on additional meaning as the ritual water of baptism.

6. *Author Portrait.* Illumination from the Dioscorides Manuscript of Anicia Juliana. Early 6th cent. (Nationalbibliothek, Vienna.) The classical personification of discovery, Heuresis, inspires the author, Dioscorides, to write a text on the medical properties of plants. All but a few early manuscripts have been lost or destroyed. This Byzantine example from the sixth century copies an older Roman version, thereby transmitting the earlier style of illustration to the medium of miniature painting at Constantinople.

7. *Jesus Before Pilate.* Illumination from the Rossano Gospels. 6th cent. (Archbishop Rossano Museum, Rossano, Italy.) The Roman influence on the early Byzantine style can be seen by comparing this work with the Dioscorides manuscript (6) or the earlier catacomb paintings (1, 3). During this period manuscript illuminations are closely related to monumental painting. In spite of the brief, cursory style there is a sense of completeness and spatial depth. Gestures and groups of overlapping figures create a feeling of dramatic tension. The manuscript may have originated in Constantinople.

8. *Madonna with Christ Child.* Encaustic icon. 6th–7th cents. St. Katerina Monastery, Mt. Sinai. This is a detail of an icon (a portable religious image) showing the Virgin with SS. Theodore and George and two angels. It is one of the earliest examples from the period in which the icon style began to crystallize. More than merely symbolic or illustrative, the icon image sought to embody sanctity or spirituality. This new aim marks a point of departure from classical goals. The same technique of encaustic had been used for the mummy portraits of Greco-Roman Egypt. Encaustic is pigment mixed with melted wax which hardens to a weather-impervious surface. It permits a building up of layers and thereby a convincing sense of modelling.

9. *St. Demetrius.* Mosaic (on a pillar). *Ca.* 629–643. Church of Hag-

ios Dimitrios, Thessalonike. A comparison with the Virgin in (8) illustrates the icon-like character of this mosaic. Art after the reign of Justinian tended toward greater flat abstraction (*cf.* 14). Holy personages are sometimes portrayed motionless and isolated, thereby approximating a cult image. It is also in this period that mosaics of such figures appear in the apse, that part of the church in which the religious ceremony takes place. Art begins to play a liturgical role.

10. *SS. Peter and Andrew Being Called by Christ.* Mosaic. Early 6th cent. Main hall, Sant' Apollinare Nuovo, Ravenna. In its depth and sense of modelling, the picture shows the abiding influence of pagan art. The mosaic is part of a series depicting the life of Christ and the Passion. Historically the series is of great interest as the earliest surviving representations of the Gospel narrative, although such subjects had been done since the fourth century.

11. *Boy with a Donkey.* Detail of floor mosaic. 5th–6th cents. Peristyle of the Great Palace of the Emperors, Istanbul. Almost nothing remains of the pictorial art of the fourth and fifth centuries in Constantinople. This rare example indicates that possibly as early as the fifth century a local school had produced art faithful to illusionism. The white background suggests space while the correctly proportioned figures are modelled in softly muted colors, all of which creates a convincing sense of naturalism.

12. *Abraham and Three Angels.* Mosaic. *Ca.* 430 A.D. Main hall wall, Santa Maria Maggiore Chapel, Rome. More than simply pictorial, portrayals of biblical events had an instructional function, and the narrative content is highly stressed. Here, three episodes are combined into a single scene.

13. *Peacock.* Mosaic detail. Early 6th cent. Choir decoration, San Vitale, Ravenna. Images of the peacock abound in early Christian art. The majestic, glowing colors appropriately evoke the splendor of heaven and the hope of a world to come. Like many contemporary themes (3) the message stresses unmediated salvation. It is only in the later Middle Ages that images of Christ on the cross stress His sacrifice as the means.

14. *Moses on Mt. Horeb.* Mosaic. Early 6th cent. South wall, Chapel of the Ceremonial Hall, San Vitale, Ravenna. Moses listens to the voice of God while removing his sandals to stand on the holy ground. God's presence is seen in the burning bush—a radiant splendor against a dark, mysterious background.

15. *Decorative geometric mosaic.* Early 5th cent. Mausoleum of Galla Placidia, Ravenna. Ravenna, capital of the Western Empire in the fifth century, was lavishly adorned with palaces and churches, where entire surfaces glowed with rich mosaic ornament. Purely decorative patterns such as this were inspired by classical prototypes.

16. *Mountains.* Detail of mosaic depicting Moses on Mt. Sinai. Early 6th cent. San Vitale, Ravenna. This detail is taken from a scene in which Moses receives the tablets of the law on Mt. Sinai. Compact blocks of strongly vibrant color convey mountainous ridges, with trees and bushes among the rocks.

17. *St. Bartholomew, the Apostle.* Mosaic. Mid-5th cent. Baptistery of the Cathedral, Ravenna. The distances between cubes were deliberately varied to create an overall suggestiveness. Color and radiance could be controlled in this manner. The art of mural mosaic, which came into bloom at the end of classical antiquity, flourished throughout the Byzantine period and seemed to have expired along with that empire.

18. *An Apostle.* Detail from wall mosaic depicting the Dormition of the Virgin. *Ca.* 1315. Church of the Holy Apostles, Thessalonike. Late medieval artists frequently based their creations on antique models. This fourteenth-century apostle is similar to that of the fifth century (17). The technique of placing the stones concentrically to suggest roundness had been used during the Roman period (11). Shadows of pale blue and green recall the nineteenth-century Impressionistic color principles. The use of contrasting color values had been employed earlier at San Vitale (14) and S. Maria Maggiore (12).

19. *St. Zacharias.* Mosaic medallion. Early 11th cent. Ceiling vault of Hosios Lucas, Greece. Each mosaic is part of an intricate and well-ordered grand program in which the impalpable realities of the Christian faith are mystically embodied in the church. The building itself represented heaven and the images helped to spell out this symbolism. Their vital role in the architecture derives more from merely "being" than from "telling." For example, in one vault Christ appears with James, His brother, traditionally the first bishop of Jerusalem, signifying He is the founder of the Christian Church. In the vault shown, Zacharias takes the place of James, indicating that Christ is to be taken as the completer of the cycle of the old Covenant.

20. *Christ in Majesty.* Mosaic. 13th cent. South gallery, Hagia Sophia, Istanbul. This is a detail from the Deësis, in which Christ is presented with Mary on His right and John on His left. The power, dignity, refinement of line, and subtle color relations indicate an exceptional artist. In the fourth and fifth centuries a youthful Christ was depicted amid the community of apostles or engaged in some specific action (10). It is only now that one finds the bearded Christ reigning alone. Some scholars have dated this from the twelfth century.

21. *The Transporting of St. Mark's Reliquary.* Mosaic. Mid-13th cent. South choir chapel, St. Mark's, Venice. The graceful, undulating waves of the ocean allow the solid gold of the background and deeper blue of the ship to show through, suggesting lightness and transparency. The fluid, rhythmic gestures of the two men taking in the sail repeat the pattern against the dramatic white shape that surrounds them. The oars on the left and angle of the mast on the right add expansive movement and extension to the neat, well-contained ship. A perfect and harmonious composition without a single extraneous line.

22. *The Baptism of Christ.* Mosaic. 1342–54. Grand chapel baptismal hall, St. Mark's, Venice. Small tesserae permit fine delineation. Graceful charm, refinement and greater narrative content mark the later Byzantine style, which lingered longest in Venice.

23. *St. George.* Wall painting. 10th cent. Church of Gueremé, Cappadocia. St. George, originally of Cappadocia, became one of the most popu-

lar of saints. He is mentioned daily in the Greek Mass. The apocryphal legend of St. George delivering the king's daughter from the power of a dragon has, in the medieval context, deep symbolic connotations of good triumphing over evil. This struggle is vividly transformed into the visual representation of St. George in the act of spearing the serpent. Already in the tenth century the act is portrayed with a solemnity and an abstract quality that conveys its symbolism. The formula repeats itself in the fourteenth century art of Serbia and Russia, possibly under Cappadocian influence (42).

24. *The Saints.* Wall painting. 9th–10th cent. Kokar Kilise, Cappadocia. An enormous wealth of mural painting has been discovered in the rock-cut chapels of Cappadocia, many of which have walls or roofs completely covered with frescos. The paintings are of great historical interest, as they present a mass of early iconographical material, largely from apocryphal sources, which survived the Iconoclast period to inspire the art of later centuries.

25. *Pietà.* Wall painting. 1164. Church of Nerez, near Skoplje, Yugoslavia. By the twelfth century, the Pietà, or mourning of the Virgin, a highly emotional theme, has been added to the usual Gospel narratives. Powerfully expressive faces, glances and gestures move the worshipper with their sorrow and deep compassion. There is also a new awareness of weight and volume, indicating a merging of the two realities, material and spiritual.

26. *The Archangel Gabriel.* Fresco. Late 12th cent. Church of St. George, near Kurbinovo, southern Yugoslavia. The more personal interpretation seen in the Nerez example (25) can also be found in the face and gesture of this angel. The most important element in Byzantine art had always been the human figure, a testimony to its strong classical heritage.

27. *The Baptism of Christ.* Wall painting. 14th cent. Church of the Peribleptos, Mistra, Greece. In the later Byzantine period, mosaics were supplanted by paintings such as this, in which the life of Christ is shown in great detail. A fixed iconography and wide dissemination of models resulted in "types" of pictures with similar compositions. Note the similarity between this Greek example and the Venetian ones (22, 23).

26

28. *St. Eufremos.* Wall painting. 1259. From a church in Boiana, Bulgaria. Bulgaria, freed from two centuries of Byzantine domination in 1186, launched a new era of building and artistic activity. However, church decoration tended to be less monumental than previous Byzantine art. Images resembled small icons. Even the paint handling of St. Eufremos is similar to that of the sixth-century icon of the Virgin from Mt. Sinai (8).

29. *St. Nicholas Saving a Ship.* Wall painting. 1602–4. Church of the Monastery of Suchevitsua, Rumania. During the last period of Byzantium, the Eastern Orthodox Church spread to Turkey, Greece, Rumania and Russia. Whereas Constantinople and other main Eastern centers are to succumb to the Turks, and the West is to be transformed by the Renaissance, these remote areas continued a post-Byzantine art as late as the seventeenth century.

30. *Cross-shaped reliquary.* Gold and cloisonné enamel. Byzantine, 6th–7th cents. (Vatican Museum, Rome.) Depicted are scenes from the early life of Christ and the Virgin, with the Nativity in the center. "Cloison" means partition or compartment. A large concavity is divided into compartments by metal strips, and powdered glass is added. The glass and metal fuse under heat to create a colorful, glass mosaic effect. The cross is hollow and intended to contain an object of sacred association.

31. *Reliquary with Crucifixion.* Cloisonné enamel on gold and silver-gilt. Byzantine, 7th–8th cent. (Metropolitan Museum of Art, New York.) Probably brought to Italy by a crusader, this reliquary was said to have contained a fragment of the True Cross.

32. *Gospel cover.* Gold, gems, pearls and enamel. 10th cent. (Biblioteca Nazionale Marciana, Venice.) A Gospel book was a rare and sacred object in itself, deserving of the most lavish embellishment, whether it be jewels or painted illumination. Compared with the earlier examples from the sixth to eighth centuries (30, 31), this tenth-century work shows greater control of the enamel technique, thereby permitting fine delineation of figure and drapery.

33. *The Baptism of Christ.* Gold, jewels and enamel. Mid-12th cent. St. Mark's, Venice. Byzantine styles, especially those originated in Constantinople, filtered into the West by means of decorated objects such as this. This scene of the Baptism is similar to those in the mosaic in St. Mark's (22) and the fresco from Mistra (27).

34. *The Prayer of Hannah.* Illumination from the Paris Psalter. Early 10th cent. (Bibliothèque Nationale, Paris.) In a mountainous landscape the prophetess Hannah gives a prayer of thanksgiving for the birth of her son Samuel. This manuscript, one of the masterpieces of the Macedonian Renaissance, closely follows a pure classical style. Although this particular page is not quite representative, we can still see perspective, cast shadows and a graceful rendering of volume in the figure and drapery.

35. *Virgin and Child.* Illumination from the Etchmiadzin Gospel, executed in the Monastery of Noravank' Siunik'. 989. (State Museum, Yerevan, Armenia.) The creative periods of Armenian art correspond to the periods of national independence. From the end of the ninth century to the beginning of the eleventh, the Bagratid kingdoms of Ari and Kars were free of Arab domination. This period corresponds to the Macedonian Renaissance in the West. The sense of antique monumentality is similar to that of the Paris Psalter (34). The pattern for this manuscript is no doubt a very early one, as the Virgin is shown in the same attitude of prayer as in the early catacomb paintings (1, 3).

36. *Illustrations of the Gospels.* Ms. illumination. Northern Italy, second half of 11th cent. (Biblioteca Palatina, Parma.) Manuscripts of this period are characterized by their brilliancy and graceful decoration. The emphasis on contour, with color seemingly filled in afterwards, causes them to resemble enamels. Depicted are: The Burial of Christ, Angels at the Tomb, The Ascension of Christ, and the Advent of the Holy Ghost.

37. *The Archangel Michael.* Illumination from the Homilies of St. John Chrysostom. *Ca.* 1078. (Bibliothèque Nationale, Paris.) The grand manner of mosaics is here transferred to a manuscript, perhaps done by monastic

artists employed in the imperial palace. The decorative style shows an influence of enamel work and figured textiles.

38. *The Crowning of David.* Illustration for the Book of Psalms. Constantinople, 1066. (British Museum, London.) The small, vivid scenes in the margins of monastic psalters contrast markedly with the lavish court style of (37). This manuscript was executed at the monastery of the Studion at Constantinople, famous for its opposition to iconoclasm during the eighth and ninth centuries.

39. *The Annunciation.* Illumination from the Gospel of 1316. Armenia. (State Museum, Yerevan, Armenia.) While Europe experienced a high point of sophisticated culture and advanced artistic styles (88, 89, 90) in the thirteenth and fourteenth centuries, Armenia, on the outskirts of civilization, maintained an art which looks several centuries older. T'oros Taronastsi executed this and a number of other manuscripts at the Monastery of Gladsor.

40. *St. Panteleimon.* Icon, encaustic over gesso on wood. Russia, 10th–11th cents. (State Museum of Fine Arts, Moscow.) Just as the relic of a saint possessed holy qualities, the image of a saint had taken on semi-divine attributes. It was against such veneration of the art object that Iconoclasm arose in the eighth century. Yet the impressive, almost awesome character of such later icons as this owes its style to previous artistic aims that sought to embody divine spirituality. This icon, a hollowed panel, shows St. Panteleimon in half length with a casket in his left hand and a stylus in his right. The technique of painting and facial type are similar to the earliest icons of the sixth century (8), which were influenced by Egyptian mummy portraits of the Roman period.

41. *Head of an Archangel.* Icon panel. School of Novgorod, 12th cent. (Russian Museum, Leningrad.) The Byzantine tradition was already active in Russia at the end of the tenth century. The Church of St. Sophia in Kiev was richly decorated with mosaics and frescos, and Kiev became one of the principal centers of the diffusion of art in Russia. From Kiev the Byzantine current reached Novgorod, where it was responsible for such twelfth-century icons as this.

42. *St. George.* Icon. 14th cent. (Russian Museum, Leiningrad.) The popular icon of St. George probably originated in Cappadocia, original birthplace of the saint (23). Here, the symbolic deed has become filled with a greater sense of immediate action. The horse rears with a graceful but lively spirit and St. George's cloak flutters with the agitation of motion.

43. *The Annunciation.* Icon panel. Byzantine, end of 14th cent. St. Clement's, Ohrid, Yugoslavia. Panel paintings are more numerous in the last century of Byzantium than during any preceding period. The panel is painted on both sides for use in processions. The reverse portrays the Virgin as Indicator of the Way (Hodegetria). Scientific and philosophic writings as well as the art during the reign of the Palaeologues prepared the way for the Italian Renaissance. Compare with (87, 88).

44. *The Annunciation.* Silk textile. East Christian, 7th–8th cents. Vatican Museum, Rome.) A classical model has been used but the stylization and pattern are Byzantine. It is assumed that such textiles were woven in Alexandria, the citadel of Hellenism. As wrappings for relics and holy objects, Byzantine silks reached Western church treasuries.

45. *Lion Pattern.* Silk textile. Byzantine, 7th–8th cents. (Vatican Museum, Rome.) Lions of the Ishtar gate in Babylon and the animals of the hunting scenes—elephants, ibexes, lions—in Sassanian rock tombs appeared in many textiles. The motifs here go back to the Sassanid Persians of the third to the seventh centuries A.D.

46. *Fibula.* Gold and precious stones. Wittislingen, Germany, 7th cent. (Bayerisches Nationalmuseum, Munich.) Metal accessories and embellished objects of personal attire such as this brooch were fashioned by most of the Germanic peoples. The origins of the style go back to the ancient Near East. The love of jewelled effects, curvilinear forms and abstract design continues in Romanesque sculptural ornament and the stained glass windows of Gothic cathedrals.

47. *Carved and painted slab.* Vallstena, Gotland, Sweden, 6th–7th cent. (Historiska Museet, Stockholm.) Complex linear designs were characteristic of the Northern tribes; human figures, as on this painted slab, are rare. The exact meaning is unclear. A similar dragon-killer armed with an ax is found on one of the plaques from Torslunda. Other stones were found at Hablingbo in Gotland and at Haeggeby, which indicates a widespread Nordic culture.

48. *The Crucifixion.* Illumination from an Irish psalter from Dover. 10th cent. (St. John's College, Cambridge.) The Celts who inhabited Ireland before the Roman conquest passed on their own tradition of ornament. The style of manuscript painting practiced in Ireland after the introduction of Christianity was once termed "Celtic," but since much similar work was done in Britain by Anglo-Saxon monks, the style is now called "Hiberno-Saxon."

49. *Symbolic representation of St. Matthew.* Illumination from the Echternach Gospels. Northumbria, early 8th cent. (Bibliothèque Nationale, Paris.) Manuscript painting became the most important and common art of the Middle Ages. It was also one of the most original forms of expression and the principal means of transmitting artistic styles. Hiberno-Saxon manuscripts were widely disseminated on the Continent by Irish monks.

50. *Virgin and Child.* Illumination from the Book of Kells. Irish, late 8th cent. (Trinity College, Dublin.) This manuscript is one of the finest examples of the Insular style. The particular composition is interesting as evidence of the veneration of the Virgin Mary in the early Irish Church. Note also the rich border writhing with fantastic serpentine forms.

51. *Decorative letters.* Illumination from the Book of Lichfield. Hiberno-Saxon, 8th cent. (Library of Lichfield Cathedral.) The large two letters are Chi and Rho (the first letters of the Greek spelling of Christ). The curvilinear bands within the letters become so intertwined and mazelike that they are impossible to trace.

52. *An Eagle, the symbol of St. John.* Illumination from the Evangelistry

of Dimma. Irish, late 8th cent. (Trinity College, Dublin.) Never logical, the ornament thrives on spontaneity juxtaposed with symmetry and contrasting colors set off by linear patterns.

53. *A Lion, the symbol of St. Mark.* Manuscript illumination. English, 1138. (British Museum, London.) Early manuscripts provide models for ones centuries later. The style of the symbols of the Evangelists is this twelfth-century English manuscript is very close to that of the Irish manuscript of the eighth century (52).

54. *Decorative letter "A."* Detail from a 12th-century English psalter. (Corpus Christi College, Cambridge.) All manner of ornamentation was used to beautify the texts. The interlocking style of this twelfth-century English letter recalls the borders and initials of the Book of Kells (50) and the Book of Lichfield (57).

55. *Decorative letter "L."* Initial letter from a Gospel manuscript. *Ca.* 1140. (Corpus Christi College, Oxford.) The fantastic creatures which appear and disappear within the decoration prefigure the marginal drolleries of fourteenth-century manuscripts. As with the gargoyles and beasts of Romanesque doorways, their exact meaning remains unclear. Sometimes they suggest legendary monsters or the lurking forces of evil, at other times they appear to be merely amusing.

56. *Decorative letters.* From the Sacramentary of Gellone. Flavigny, late 8th cent. (Bibliothèque Nationale, Paris.) This sacramentary gives us an indication of a manuscript style on the Continent before the diffusion of Anglo-Irish art.

57. *A Scholar of the Gospel of Matthew.* Illumination from the Cutbercht Gospels. Salzburg. *Ca.* 770. (Staatsbibliothek, Vienna.) The English monk Cutbercht wrote this manuscript in Salzburg, the ecclesiastical center of a large area covering modern Bavaria and parts of Austria. Salzburg was also an important school of illumination. Early manuscripts such as this show strong Insular elements.

58. *Scenes from Genesis.* Manuscript page from the Ashburnham Penta-teuch. 7th cent. (Bibliothèque Nationale, Paris.) The scenes, probably painted in northern Italy, illustrate the five books of Moses. The small pictures present a genre-like realism with vivid movement, far removed from both Byzantine formality and the wild patterns of Hiberno-Saxon painting. Certain elements such as the spirited action prefigure a later Romanesque style. In the first register are depicted: Adam and Eve, and the offerings of Cain and Abel (the presence of God is represented by a hand thrust from a cloud). In the second: Cain ploughing and questioned by God. In the third: The killing of Abel.

59. *St. John.* Illumination from the Evangelistry of Godescalc. 781–783. (Bibliothèque Nationale, Paris.) Under Charlemagne, a complex congeries of traditions, such as Celtic, Viking or Oriental, combine against a background of Byzantine and Roman styles. This page gives us a portrait of the author seated with his book in the manner of the Roman Dioscorides manuscript (6). The facial type and monumental pose against a gold background are Byzantine (14, 19, 20). Yet the agitation, linear quality and especially the interlace border derive from Hiberno-Saxon art (48–51).

60. *St. Matthew.* Illumination from the Gospel book of Otto III. Reich-enau School. *Ca.* 1000. (Bayerische Staatsbibliothek, Munich.) Ottonian artists transformed the Carolingian style into one of dramatic spiritual expression, with accentuated gestures, imposing facial expression and a more monumental form. Here again is an author portrait as in the Carolingian example (59), but now the Evangelist is an ecstatic visionary. As if charged with divine electricity, he sits in a mystic cloud peopled with prophets, kings and angels to symbolize the New Testament proceeding from the Old.

61. *Otto III Enthroned.* Illumination from the Gospel book of Otto III. *Ca.* 1000. (Bayerische Staatsbibliothek, Munich.) The Ottonian emperors continued the political aims of the Carolingians. With the staff in his right hand and the globe in his left, Otto rules the political and religious realms in the Byzantine tradition of Justinian. The political relationship with Byzantium had been strengthened by Otto II's marriage to the Greek princess Theofano.

62. *St. Fides.* Gold and enamel. Early 12th cent. (Church treasury of Sainte-Foy, Conques, France.) The cults of local martyrs and saints resulted in travel and artistic diffusion along the pilgrimage routes.

63. *Madonna.* Detail of Madonna and Child. Enamel. Early 13th cent. San Miguel de Excelsis (Navarra), northern Spain. The Virgin holds the Christ Child on her lap. Her head, parts of her body and the child were done in metal cast separately and added to the enamelled plaque. At Limoges and in the Mosan area a technique was developed, called *champlevé,* whereby the hollows were cut out of the metal ground instead of being formed by flat metal strips inserted edgewise into a incised design, as in the cloisonné technique of Byzantine enamels (30–33).

64. *Christ in Majesty.* Manuscript cover from Limoges. Gilded copper and champlevé enamel. (Musée de Cluny, Paris.) The Mosan school centering around Cologne produced a large number of outstanding enamel objects; however, the most prolific school was that of Limoges, whose liturgical objects were exported to all parts of Europe. Christ is enthroned on the arc of heaven surrounded by the symbols of the Evangelists and the letters Alpha and Omega.

65. *The Resurrection of Christ.* Enamel shoulder pad. Late 12th cent. (Louvre, Paris.) Mosan metalwork had a tradition of organic classical naturalism from Rainier of Huy (early 12th century) through Nicholas of Verdun (end of 12th century), which strongly influenced Gothic monumental sculpture. The relaxed, fluid line of this example from Wladimir Cathedral is closer to the style of a thirteenth-century stained glass window (82) than to more contemporary painting of the twelfth century (69 or 76).

66. *The Host of God.* Illumination from Beatus's Commentary on the Apocalypse. *Ca.* 1086. Cathedral of Burgo de Osma, Spain. The refined decorative flavor of the Middle East appears in Mozarabic art, the Christian art of Moslem Spain. The highly sophisticated Moslem civilization had a considerable influence on Medieval Europe. Islamic courts were great centers of learning, where philosophers and mathematicians continued the study of Aris-

totle and Euclid, and Arab libraries preserved much ancient Greek and Roman literature that had been lost in the West.

67. *Stars Falling from Heaven.* Illumination from the St. Sever Apocalypse. Mid-11th cent. (Bibliothèque Nationale, Paris.) The Mozarabic illuminators developed a primitive but highly original and colorful style which was to influence Southern French miniature painting in the early eleventh century. The inventiveness can be seen in this very unusual depiction of the Last Judgment. The stars of heaven resemble those from the Spanish Beatus Manuscript (66). The gestures and different-colored backgrounds recall the Ashburnham Pentateuch (58).

68. *Detail of St. Aubin's Miracle.* Illumination from the Life of St. Aubin. France, late 11th cent. (Bibliothèque Nationale, Paris). The flourishing of art in all areas and media during the eleventh century owed a great deal to the artistic forms established during the Carolingian and Ottonian periods. Often, as in this example, Carolingian figure types and gestures have been treated with new Romanesque vigor.

69. *The Crucifixion.* Detail of manuscript illumination. *Ca.* 1170–1183. (Bodleian Library, Oxford.) Romanesque directness, tenderness and simplicity are evident.

70. *The Resurrection of the Dead.* Illumination from the Vyšehrad Gospel book. 1080–1090. (Prague National University Library.) The Western art of France, Lorraine and England penetrated as far as Bohemia. This Gospel book has many stylistic points of contact with the art of Cluny (France) of about the same period.

71. *Dedication of a Church.* Detail of a fresco. *Ca.* 1255. Crypt of the cathedral of Anagni, Italy. Romanesque painting in Italy draws upon a Byzantine heritage. The figures here recall a stable monumentality of an earlier period. This painting is a visual document of the consecration of the church which took place after the Bishop of Anagni had placed within it some highly venerated relics.

72. *The Archangel Michael and Angels Battle a Dragon.* Fresco. *Ca.* 1100. Porch of Saint-Savin-sur-Gartempe (Vienne), France. Owing much to the agitation and expressive line of Carolingian art, particularly the Reims school, these frescos capture a fluid sense of action. With a minimum of brushwork, the forms are suggested, without backgrounds. The paintings are somewhat damaged, and originally the entire church had been adorned with frescos. This loose French Romanesque style contrasts markedly with the more static Byzantine-influenced Italian style (71).

73. *Personification of Lust and Despair.* Fresco. Early 12th cent. Crypt of the Church of Tavant (Indre-et-Loire), France. This image combines a traditional representation of Despair, a woman killing herself, with that of Lust, a woman with serpents attached to her breasts. There are other signs of abbreviation in the cycle of the Tavant crypt. The pictures appear to be a selection from a larger, more fully developed sequence. As in St.-Savin-sur-Gartempe the sketch-like spontaneity and vivid dynamism hark back to the Reims school of the Carolingian period.

74. *The Horses of the Magi.* Detail of painted wooden ceiling. Mid-12th cent. Church of Saint-Martin, Zillis (Grisons), Switzerland. The diversity of Romanesque styles and media is again indicated by this painted ceiling. Paintings on wood may have been more numerous, but relatively few have survived. The cursive yet disciplined line is usually used in stained glass rather than in murals or manuscripts.

75. *St. Mary and St. John.* Fresco. *Ca.* 1150. From the apse of San Pedro de la Seo de Urel. (Museum of Catalan Art, Barcelona.) Despite the flatness, there is stable form and solid monumentality here which recalls the solemn sanctity and intangible spirituality of Byzantine art. The style parallels developments in Italy. San Pedro de Urgel is one of many churches in Catalonia with a similar style of frescos.

76. *Madonna in Glory with Christ Child.* Painted wood. Second half of 12th cent. Frontal of an altar dedicated to St. Margaret. (Museo Episcopal,

Vich, Barcelona, Spain.) Images of the Madonna and Child become more numerous as the Virgin took on a greater importance in the religion of the twelfth century.

77. *The Beheading of St. Margaret.* Painted wood. Second half of 12th cent. Frontal of an altar dedicated to St. Margaret. (Museo Episcopal, Vich, Barcelona, Spain.) The assured, knowing firmness bears the imprint of a vivid spirit and an immediacy conveyed without hesitation. In Romanesque art there is a linear vivacity and dynamism of style which may be traced back through the art of the Ottonians (60), Carolingians (59), Saxons and Irish (48–52) to the art of the northern barbaric peoples (46, 47).

78. *A Knight.* Detail of Tapestry from Baldishol. 12th cent. (Kunstindustrimuseet, Oslo.) Originally the tapestry depicted all twelve months, reaching a length of about 39 ft. It is of a pure northern style, and one of several hangings similar to the Bayeux Tapestry (79), which suggests that the Bayeux work derives from a Norse or Scandinavian tradition.

79. *The Ship of Prince Harold.* Detail from the Bayeux Tapestry. *Ca.* 1080. (Bayeux Museum, Normandy.) The tapestry has great historical importance as one of the principal contemporary accounts of the Norman conquest of England. No other work of this kind has survived from such an early period of the Middle Ages. The embroidery, worked on coarse linen in woolen thread, achieves an effect that is strikingly ornamental. As the scenes unfold, a current runs through them of excitement, drama and exuberant festivity. It was made at the direction of Odo of Bayeux for display in the new cathedral dedicated in 1077.

80. *A Cask-maker* (*Donor's portrait*). Stained glass. 1210–1220. Chartres Cathedral. Suger, the abbot of St. Denis who built one of the first and finest Gothic structures, wrote that the windows would "direct thought by material means toward that which is immaterial." The beautifully colored glow of light from the windows was symbolically associated with the divine radiance of the Lord. Each change in color is represented by an individual fragment of glass held in place by a framework of soldered lead. Features and designs were

painted on with a warm gray-brown paint which contained powdered glass. When fired, the design fused with the glass.

81. *A Cloth-maker (Donor's Portrait)*. Stained glass. 1210–1212. Chartres Cathedral. Chartres still possesses most of its original glass, which is famous for its deep, brilliant blue. All of the windows were paid for by various members of the local society, from kings to craftsmen. During the early thirteenth century, the workshop of Chartres Cathedral was the most important center for stained glass in France.

82. *The Prophet Ezekiel*. Stained glass. *Ca*. 1225. (Victoria and Albert Museum, London.) Unlike Romanesque art, which differed widely in style according to location or medium, the Gothic style, in all media, was rapidly diffused throughout Europe, giving an international character to Gothic art. English drawings such as this resembled the finest in France, and there was a constant interchange between stained-glass drawings and manuscript illuminations.

83. *November*. Stained glass detail. Early 13th cent. South rose window of the Cathedral of Lausanne. Divine order could be seen in nature, where life is regulated by the changing seasons. The place of man in God's creation was clearly defined and every month had its proper activities. Frequently the Labors of the Months give us a genre-like view of medieval daily life. Livestock are slaughtered in the month of November, just as courtly activities mark the month of May (78).

84. *Rose Window*. *Ca*. 1260–80. South transept, Notre Dame, Paris. Stained-glass windows had become an organic part of the architecture. Builders sought ways to create increasingly slender masonry supports. Entire walls came to radiate a jewelled brilliance. And as no direct light would penetrate the building, there was an even glow of pervasive harmony to the interior light.

85. *The Stream of Life*. Detail from the Tapestry of Angers. By Jean de Bondol (Hennequin de Bruges) and Nicolas Bataille. *Ca*. 1381. (Musée des Tapisseries, Angers.) The lower portion of this detail shows the Stream

of Life, which flows from the heavenly throne of God, as described in Revelations. The tapestry was inspired by an illuminated manuscript, an Apocalypse lent by Charles V to his brother. There are seven hangings, each about 65½ ft. long.

86. *Beast of the Apocalypse.* Detail from the Tapestry of Angers. By Jean de Bondol (Hennequin de Bruges) and Nicolas Bataille. *Ca.* 1381. (Musée des Tapisseries, Angers.) The evocative power of the Scriptures is enriched by the imagination of the artist. Throughout the tapestry there is a limited and austere range of colors and designs of great simplicity and linear clarity.

87. *St. Francis Preaching to the Birds.* Detail of an altar painting by Bonaventura Berlinghieri. 1235. Church of San Francesco, Pescia. A large image of St. Francis is surrounded by small scenes from his life. The mendicant order of the Franciscans, who preached among the people with a simple, direct approach, inspired an upsurge of popular religious feeling. The naive charm of this scene conveys the simple immediacy of St. Francis.

88. *Birth of the Virgin.* Detail of an altar painting by the Master of San Martino. Late 13th cent. (Museo Nazionale, Pisa.) Byzantine influence was especially strong in Pisa and Lucca during the late thirteenth century. Figures draped in classical garments appear with a sense of weight and volume not seen for hundreds of years.

89. *Abraham and the Three Angels.* Illumination from the St. Louis Psalter. 1253–70. (Bibliothèque Nationale, Paris.) The scenes reflect contemporary clothes and architecture. Artists of the royal workshop may also have worked on stained-glass windows. By the mid-thirteenth century there is a widely expanded production of books and manuscripts for all purposes. Private devotional books were especially numerous.

90. *Summer Landscape.* Illumination from the Carmina Burana manuscript. Early 13th cent. (Staatsbibliothek, Munich.) Expansion of the urban universities accompanied a revival of learning of all kinds, classical literature

as well as studies of the natural world. Secular manuscripts increased and this is one of the first to be illustrated with miniatures. The exuberant joy in nature seems to burst from both the verses and the painting.

91. *Lovers.* Illumination from the Manesse manuscript. *Ca.* 1320. (Heidelberg University Library.) The growth of court patronage in the thirteenth century (89), which had inclined the late Medieval style toward greater refinement and fashionable elegance, becomes still more predominant in the fourteenth century. The manuscript is a collection of poems by various German knights from the middle of the twelfth until the first half of the fourteenth centuries. This picture was suggested by a love song sung to his lady by Konrad von Alstetten. Court life centering around chivalric love became a dominant theme of the later Middle Ages.

THE PLATES

1
Veiled Orant. Wall painting. *Ca.* 220–40 A.D. Catacomb of St. Priscilla, Rome. The earliest Christian images were executed in the style and technique of Roman wall painting.

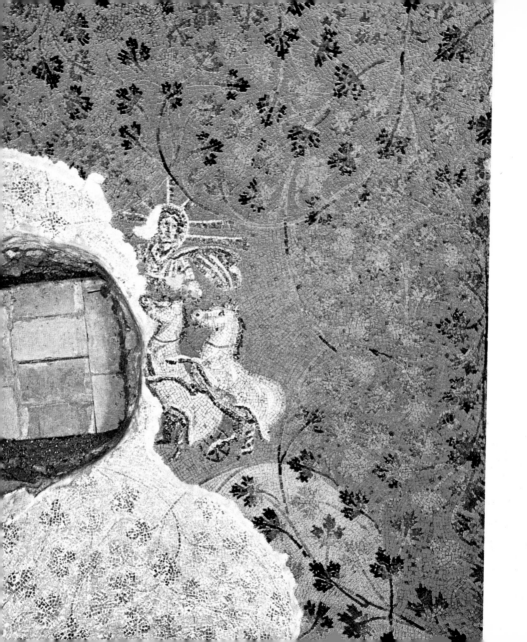

3 *Three Youths in the Furnace.* Wall painting. 3rd–4th cents. A.D. Catacomb of St. Priscilla, Rome. Such Old Testament themes were believed to prefigure Christ's Resurrection.

←2 *Christ as Apollo the Sun God (Christos Helios).* Mosaic. 3rd cent. A.D. Necropolis under St. Peter's, Rome. Christ became the new symbol of divine radiance and rebirth.

4 *Coptic textile with Dionysos,* 4th–6th cents. A.D. (Kunsthistorisches Museum, Vienna.)
Christian Egypt clung to classical themes and ancient ornamental abstraction.

5 *Coptic textile with Figures and Fish.* 4th–6th cents. A.D. (Louvre, Paris.) Colorful, decorative textiles are the finest products of Coptic art.

6   *Author Portrait*. Illumination from the Dioscorides Manuscript of Anicia Juliana. Early 6th cent. (Nationalbibliothek, Vienna.)   The muse Discovery inspires the author.

7   *Jesus Before Pilate*. Illumination from the Rossano Gospels. 6th cent. (Archbishop Ros- →
sano Museum, Rossano, Italy.)   Pilate asks the crowd which prisoner should be released, Jesus or Barabbas.

ѠΝΔΕΠΙΛΑΤΟϹΟΤΙΕΚΤΗϹΕΞΟΥϹΙΑϹΗΡѠΔΟΥΕϹΤΙΝΑΝΕΠΕΜΨΕΝΑΥΤΟ
ΗΡѠΔΗΝΟΝΤΑΚΑΙΑΥΤΟΝΕΝΙΕΡΟϹΟΛΥΜΟΙϹΕΝΤΑΥΤΑΙϹΤΑΙϹΗΜΕΡΑΙϹ

ΒΑΡΑΒ
ΒΑϹ

8
Madonna with Christ Child. Encaustic icon. 6th–7th cents. St. Katerina Monastery, Mt. Sinai. A rare work of exceptional quality—serene monumentality, tenderness, and an alluring suggestion of otherworldliness.

9
St.
Demetrius.
Mosaic (on
a pillar).
Ca.
629–643.
Church of
Hagios
Dimitrios,
Thessa-
lonike.
The tran-
scendental
gaze and
lack of
volume cre-
ate an
ethereal
spirituality,
removed
from time
and space.

10
*SS. Peter and Andrew
Being Called by Christ.*
Mosaic. Early 6th
cent. Main hall, Sant'-
Apollinare Nuovo, Ra-
venna. Gold and
brightly colored mosaics
served the dual purpose
of decorating the church
and instructing the faithful.

11 *Boy with a Donkey*.   Detail of floor mosaic.   5th–6th cents.   Peristyle of the Great Palace of the Emperors, Istanbul.   The naturalism and non-religious subject matter are pure Roman.

12 *Abraham and Three Angels.* Mosaic. *Ca.* 430 A.D. Main hall wall, Santa Maria Maggiore
Chapel, Rome. The brilliant colors and narrative content herald a new tone.

13
Peacock. Mosaic detail.
Early 6th cent. Choir decoration, San Vitale, Ravenna.
The peacock was a symbol
of paradise and immortality
of the soul.

14
Moses on Mt. Horeb.
Mosaic. Early 6th cent.
South wall, Chapel of the
Ceremonial Hall, San Vitale,
Ravenna. Cubes of gold and
dazzling color reflect the
light of a divine eminence. →

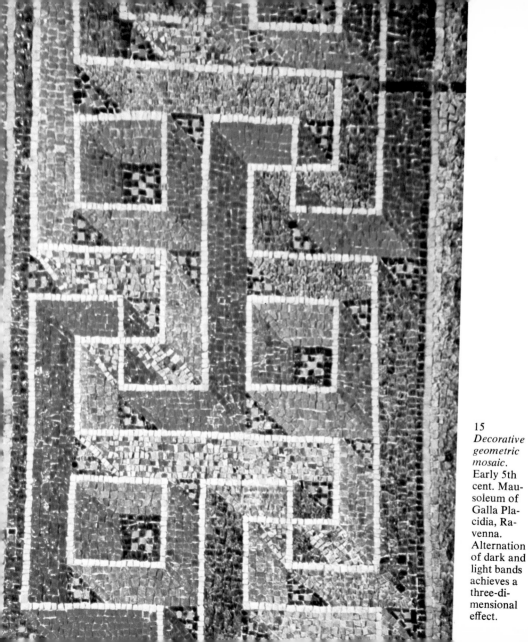

15
Decorative geometric mosaic. Early 5th cent. Mausoleum of Galla Placidia, Ravenna. Alternation of dark and light bands achieves a three-dimensional effect.

16
Mountains. Detail of mosaic depicting Moses on Mt. Sinai. Early 6th cent. San Vitale, Ravenna. Subtle and greatly varied tones create the rich style of Justinian's art.

17
St. Bartholomew, the Apostle. Mosaic. Mid-5th cent. Baptistery of the Cathedral, Ravenna. Light and shade are of little concern—the wall itself seems aglow.

18
An Apostle.
Detail from
wall mosaic
depicting the
Dormition of
the Virgin.
Ca. 1315.
Church of
the Holy
Apostles,
Thessaloníke.
Later artists
strove for
greater emo-
tional depth.

19
St. Zacharias. Mosaic medallion. Early 11th cent. Ceiling vault of Hosios Lucas, Greece. Each picture derives its importance and sanctity from its location.

20
Christ in Majesty. Mosaic. 13th cent. South gallery, Hagia Sophia, Istanbul. Awesome grandeur and refined technique. One of the greatest masterpieces of Byzantine art.

21 *The Transporting of St. Mark's Reliquary*. Mosaic. Mid-13th cent. South choir chapel, St. Mark's, Venice. Graceful decorativeness and simple charm belie the ingeniously subtle composition.

22 *The Baptism of Christ*. Mosaic. 1342–54. Grand chapel baptismal hall, St. Mark's, → Venice. Refinement of detail typified the Venetian style.

23 *St. George.* Wall painting. 10th cent. Church of Gueremé, Cappadocia. This is one of the earliest images of this saint.

24 *The Saints*.   Wall painting.   9th–10th cents.   Kokar Kilise, Cappadocia.   The rock-cut
churches reveal a primitive but vigorous monastic art.

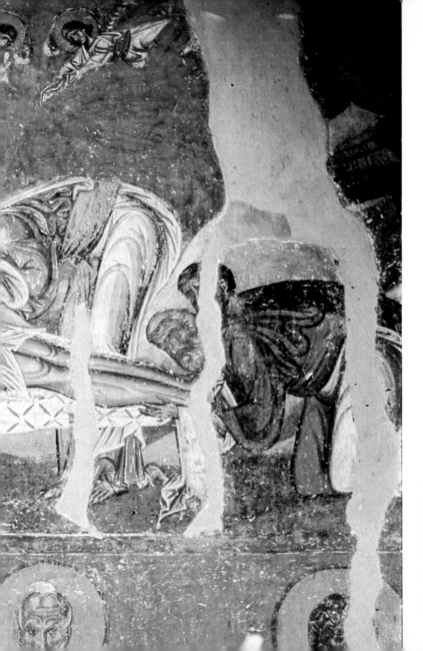

25
Pietà. Wall
painting. 1164.
Church of
Nerez, near
Skoplje, Yugo-
slavia. Deep
tenderness
and poignant
emotion add a
new human
dimension to
Byzantine art.

26
The Archangel Gabriel.
Fresco.
Late 12th
cent.
Church
of St.
George,
near Kurbinovo,
southern
Yugoslavia.
An agitated, linear liveliness
combined
with a
dignified
monumentality.

27
The Baptism of Christ.
Wall painting. 14th cent. Church of the Periblep- tos, Mistra, Greece. Delicacy and re- finement charac- terize the last pe- riod of Byzantine art.

28 *St. Eufremos.* Wall painting. 1259. From a church in Boiana, Bulgaria. Like an icon, the saint is painted with bold directness.

29 *Saint Nicholas Saving a Ship.* Wall painting. 1602–4. Church of the Monstery of Suche- →
vitsua, Rumania. The charming narrative treatment of the last Byzantine style lingered in outlying countries.

ПЛ҃ВѢ СТГО НИКОЛЫ В ЗКО
РАБЛЕ

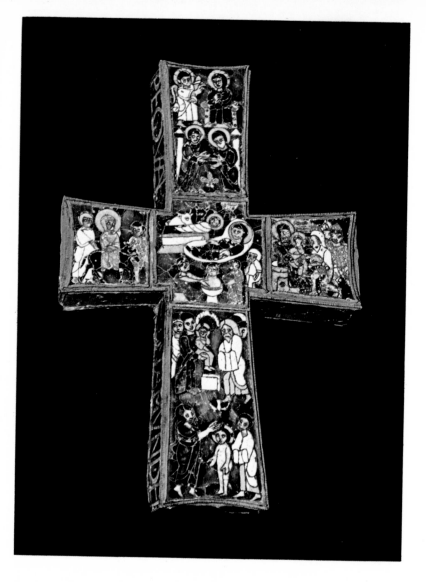

30 *Cross-shaped reliquary.* Gold and cloisonné enamel. Byzantine, 6th–7th cents. (Vatican Museum, Rome.) The enamel technique provides a surface for colorful pictorial art.

31 *Reliquary with Crucifixion.* Cloisonné enamel on gold and silver-gilt. Byzantine, 7th–8th cents. (Metropolitan Museum of Art, New York.) Simplified figures seem suited to the rich, jewelled effect.

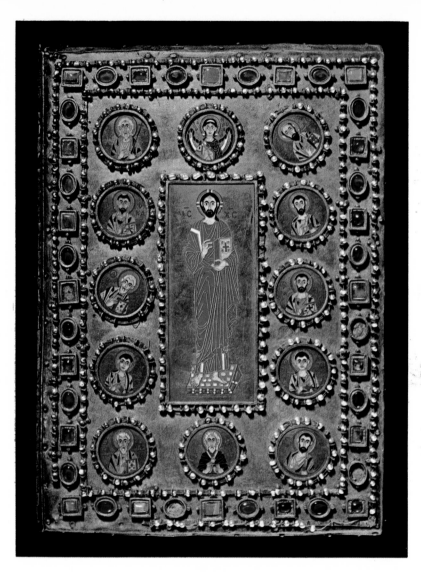

32 *Gospel cover*.   Gold, gems, pearls and enamel.   10th cent.   (Biblioteca Nazionale Marciana, Venice.)   Objects such as this reflect the magnificence of work produced at Constantinople.

33 *The Baptism of Christ.* Gold, jewels and enamel. Mid-12th cent. St. Mark's, Venice. Portable works helped spread the Byzantine style to the West.

34 *The Prayer of Hannah*.   Illumination from the Paris Psalter.   Early 10th cent.   (Bibliothèque Nationale, Paris.)   Classical tactile values reappear during the Macedonian Renaissance.

35 *Virgin and Child.* Illumination from the Etchmiadzin Gospel, executed in the Monastery of Norabank' Siunik'. 989 A.D. (State Museum, Yerevan, Armenia.) Severe monumentality combined with tender naiveté.

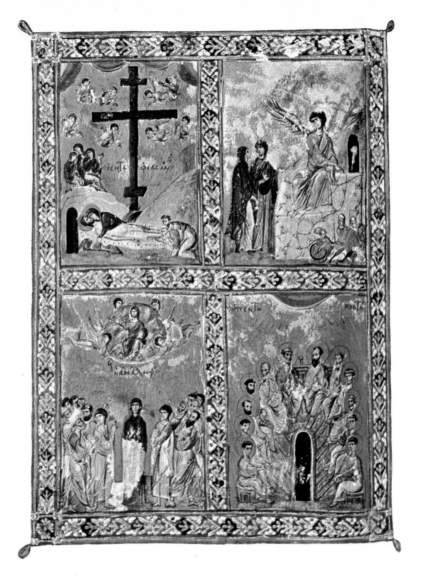

36 *Illustrations of the Gospels.* Ms. illumination, Northern Italy, second half of 11th cent. (Biblioteca Palatina, Parma.) The delicate brilliancy resembles that of cloisonné enamels.

37
The Archangel Michael. Illumination from the Homilies of St. John Chrysostom. *Ca.* 1078. (Bibliothèque Nationale, Paris.) Court tastes favored lavish ornamentation and exotic techniques.

38 *The Crowning of David.*   Illustration for the Book of Psalms.   Constantinople, 1066.   (British Museum, London.)   Such marginal illustrations were common in monastic psalters.

39 *The Annunciation.*   Illumination from the Gospel of 1316.   Armenia.   (State Museum, Yerevan, Armenia.)   Armenia retained its early directness of narrative and ornamentation.

40
*St. Pantalei-
mon.* Icon,
encaustic
over gesso
on wood.
Russia,
10th–11th
cents. (State
Museum of
Fine Arts,
Moscow.)
As holy im-
ages, icons
were meant
to embody a
solemn sanc-
tity.

41 *Head of an Archangel.* Icon panel. School of Novgorod, 12th cent. (Russian Museum, Leningrad.) In Russia, the Byzantine tradition is best represented by icons.

42 *St. George.* Icon. 14th cent. (Russian Museum, Leningrad.) The cult of St. George, as patron saint of soldiers, spread to the West during the crusades.

43 *The Annunciation.* Icon panel. Byzantine, end of 14th cent. St. Clement's, Ohrid, Yugoslavia. One of the finest paintings of late Byzantine art.

44 *The Annunciation.* Silk textile. East Christian, 7th–8th cents. (Vatican Museum, Rome.)
Byzantine influences were particularly evident in the textile arts.

45 *Lion pattern.* Silk textile. Byzantine, 7th–8th cents. (Vatican Museum, Rome.) Many →
Byzantine silks borrowed Iranian or Oriental motifs.

46 *Fibula.* Gold and precious stones. Wittislingen, Germany, 7th cent. (Bayerisches Nationalmuseum, Munich.) Decorative metalwork is the predominant art of the Germanic
migratory peoples.

47
*Carved and painted
slab.* Vallstena,
Gotland, Sweden,
6th–7th cents.
(Historiska Museet,
Stockholm.) Strange
designs or symbols
are flanked by
dragons and heroes
from the Nordic
sagas.

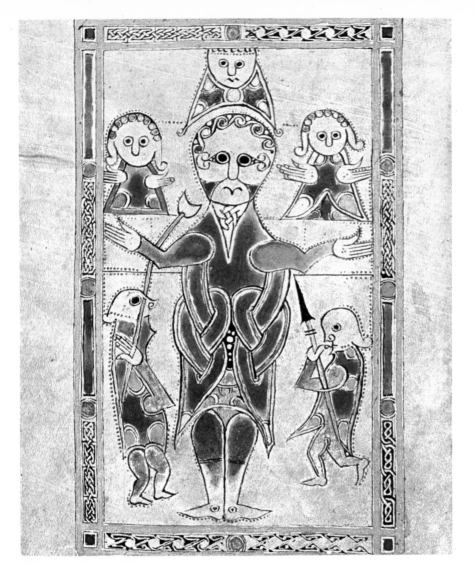

48 *The Crucifixion.* Illumination from an Irish psalter from Dover. 10th cent. (St. John's College, Cambridge.) The barbaric tradition of abstract design is applied to Christian themes.

49 *St. Matthew.* Illumination from the Echternach Gospels. Northumbria, early 8th cent. (Bibliothèque Nationale, Paris.) The body of the saint is converted to a decorative symbol.

50
*Virgin and
Child*. Illum-
ination from
the Book of
Kells. Irish,
late 8th cent.
(Trinity Col-
lege, Dub-
lin.) Like
jewelry, the
entire page
sparkles with
a profusion
of ornament.

51
Decorative letters. Illumination from the Book of Lichfield. Hiberno-Saxon, 8th cent. (Library of Lichfield Cathedral.) The initial of each page is usually enlarged and embellished.

52 *An Eagle, the symbol of St. John.* Illumination from the Evangelistry of Dimma. Irish late 8th cent. (Trinity College, Dublin.) A tradition of animal ornament found its favorite subjects in such symbols.

53 *A Lion, the symbol of St. Mark.* Manuscript illumination. English, 1138. (British Museum, London.) Liveliness is created by the combination of symmetry and asymmetry.

54 *Decorative letter "A"*. From a 12th-century psalter. (Corpus Christi College, Cambridge.) Hiberno-Saxon interlace style continued in English manuscripts after the Norman Conquest.

55
Decorative letter "L". From a Gospel manuscript. *Ca.* 1140. (Corpus Christi College, Oxford.) Ornaments become imaginary creatures and turn again into decoration.

iber g̃
ihū xp̄i
Abɪah
Isaac a
Autem: ge
lũdar h̃ gl
dechtmah. pl
Cmom h̃: ghnitɪ
Ammɪtɔab. Ammɪtɔab h̃: z

56
Decorative letters. From the Sacramentary of Gellone. Flavigny, late 8th cent. (Bibliothèque Nationale, Paris.) Oriental and Byzantine traditions are evident here.

57 *A Scholar of the Gospel of Matthew.* Illumination from the Cutbercht Gospels. Salzburg, *ca.* 770. (Staatsbibliothek, Vienna.) An example of the Hiberno-Saxon influence transported to the Continent.

58 *Scenes from Genesis.*   Manuscript page from the Ashburnham Pentateuch.   7th cent.
(Bibliothèque Nationale, Paris.)   A very early precursor of the Romanesque style.

59 *St. John.* Illumination from the Evangelistry of Godescalc. 781–783. (Bibliothèque Nationale, Paris.) Commissioned by Charlemagne to commemorate his visit to Rome, Easter, 781.

60. *St. Matthew.* Illumination from the Gospel book of Otto III. Reichenau School, *ca.* 1000. (Bayerische Staatsbibliothek, Munich.) The Reichenau style tended toward simplicity of line and color.

61 *Otto III Enthroned*. Illumination from the Gospel book of Otto III. The emperor is shown reigning over both the spiritual and political realms.

62 *St. Fides.* Gold and enamel. Early 12th cent. (Church treasury of Sainte-Foy, Conques, France.) Byzantine enamel techniques spread throughout Europe.

63 *Madonna.* Detail of Madonna and Child. Gold sculpture and enamel. Early 13th cent. → (San Miguel de Excelsis, Navarra, northern Spain.)

64
Christ in Majesty. Manuscript cover from Limoges. Gilded copper and champlevé enamel. 1170–80. (Musée de Cluny, Paris.) The art of enamel work reached its peak in the 12th and 13th centuries.

65 *The Resurrection of Christ.* Enamel shoulder pad. Late 12th cent. (Louvre, Paris.) Enamel artists of the Mosan area showed an advanced sculptural naturalness.

66 *The Host of God.* Illumination from Beatus's Commentary on the Apocalypse. *Ca.* 1086. Cathedral of Burgo de Osma, Spain. Some Spanish art showed Islamic influence.

67 *Stars Falling from Heaven*. Illustration from the St. Sever Apocalypse. Mid-11th cent. (Bibliothèque Nationale, Paris.) The monastery derives its fame from this manuscript.

68 *Detail of St. Aubin's Miracle.* Illumination from the Life of St. Aubin. France, late 11th cent. (Bibliothèque Nationale, Paris.) The Aubin manuscript reflects Carolingian manuscripts from Tours.

69
*The Cru-
cifixion.*
Detail of
manus-
cript illu-
mination.
a. 1170–
1183.
Bodleian
Library,
Oxford.)
A bold-
ness of
line and
color is
ined to a
tender,
gentle
grace.

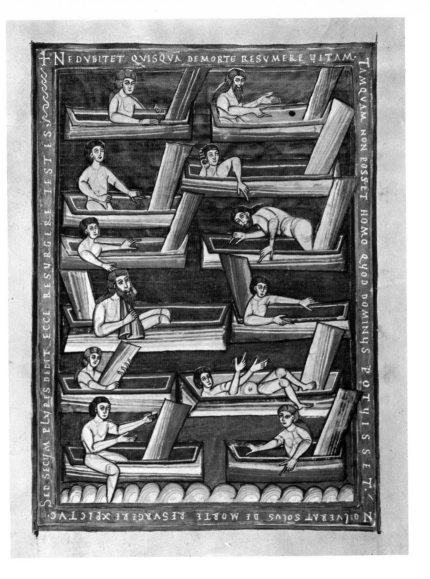

70 *The Resurrection of the Dead.* Illumination from the Vyšehrad Gospel Book. 1080–1090. (Prague National University Library.) A charming and naive depiction of this theme.

71
Dedication of a Church. Detail of a fresco. *Ca.* 1255. Crypt of the Cathedral of Anagni, Italy. A local Byzantine heritage continues in Italy.

72   *The Archangel Michael and Angels Battle a Dragon.*   Fresco.   *Ca.* 1100.   Porch of Saint-Savin-sur-Gartempe, Vienne, France.   Graceful swirls of light and pure color mark these as among the most inspired and elegant of Romanesque frescos.

73   *Personification of Lust and Despair.*   Fresco.   Early 12th cent.   Crypt of the Church of →
Tavant, Indre-et-Loire, France.   Such graphic illustrations acted as pictorial sermons.

74 *The Horses of the Magi.* Detail of a painted wooden ceiling. Mid-12th cent. Church of Saint-Martin, Zillis, Switzerland. One of 115 panels depicting scenes from the life of Christ.

75 *St. Mary and St. John.* Fresco. *Ca.* 1150. From the apse of San Pedro de la Seo de → Urgel. (Museum of Catalan Art, Barcelona.)

76
*Madonna in
Glory with
Christ Child*

77
*The Beheading
of St. Mar-
garet*

Painted wood
panels. 12th
century.
Frontal
of altar dedi-
cated to St.
Margaret.
(Museo Epis-
copal, Vich,
Barcelona.)
The firm di-
rectness of
form and spirit
is character-
istic of
Romanesque
art.

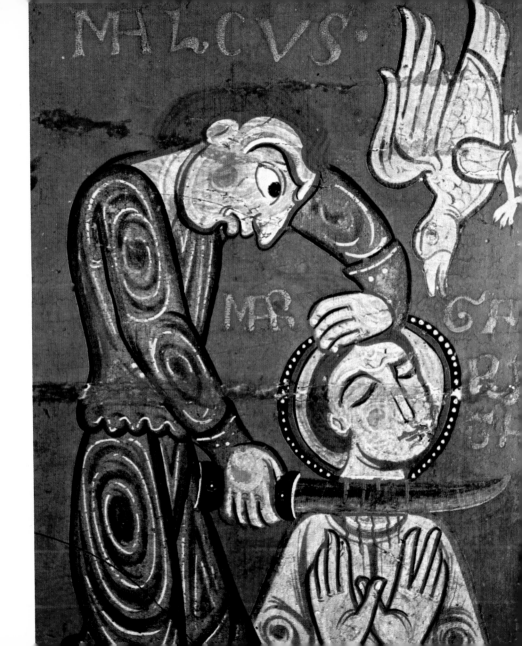

78 *A Knight*. Detail of the Tapestry from Baldishol. 12th cent. (Kunstindustrimuseet, Oslo.)
The knight represents the courtly activities which occur in the month of May.

79 *The Ship of Prince Harold*. Detail from the Bayeux Tapestry. *Ca.* 1080. (Bayeux →
Museum, Normandy.) This famous tapestry includes an account of the Battle of Hastings.

80 (Previous page), 81 (Above). *Donors' portraits from Chartres.* Stained glass. 1210–1220. Chartres Cathedral. The art of making stained-glass windows reached its peak in this period.

82 *The Prophet Ezekiel.* Stained glass. *Ca.* 1150. (Victoria and Albert Museum, London.)→

83 *November*. Stained-glass detail. Early 13th century. South rose window of the Cathedral at Lausanne. The richness of effect lies in the subtle balance and harmony of colors.

84 *Rose Window*. *Ca.* 1260–80. South transept, Notre Dame, Paris. The radiance of the windows symbolized the splendors of heaven and eternal bliss.

85
*The Stream
of Life.*
Detail
from the
Tapestry
of Angers.
Ca. 1381.
(Musée de
Tapisserie,
Angers.)
One of the
most out-
standing ex-
amples of
the tapes-
tries of the
later Mid-
dle Ages.

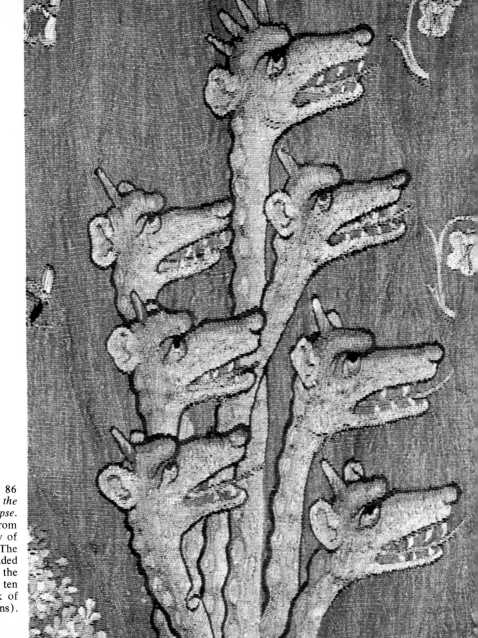

86
Beast of the Apocalypse. Detail from the Tapestry of Angers. The seven-headed beast from the sea with ten horns (Book of Revelations).

88 *Birth of the Virgin.* Detail of altar painting by the Master of San Martino. Late 13th cent. (Museo Nazionale, Pisa.) Through Byzantine influence classical standards were introduced to a Western tradition that is to culminate in the Renaissance of the 15th century.

← 87 *St. Francis Preaching to the Birds.* Detail of an altar painting by Bonaventura Berlinghieri. 1235. Church of San Francesco, Pescia. A Byzantine style acquires a new vitality in Italy.

89 *Abraham and the Three Angels.* Illumination from the St. Louis Psalter. 1253–70. (Bibliothèque Nationale, Paris.) An example of High Gothic style, influenced by royal tastes.

90 *Summer Landscape.*   Illumination from the Carmina Burana manuscript.   Early 13th cent.
(Staatsbibliothek, Munich.)   One of the first landscapes since late classical times.

91
Lovers. Illumination from the Manesse manuscript. *Ca.* 1320. (Heidelberg University Library.) The fashionable elegance of the later Middle Ages is represented by this illustrated collection of love songs.